Facts About Countries
The Caribbean

Ian Graham

FRANKLIN WATTS
LONDON•SYDNEY

First published in 2005 by
Franklin Watts
96 Leonard Street, London
EC2A 4XD

Franklin Watts Australia
Level 17/207 Kent Street
Sydney NSW 2000

Facts About Countries is based on the Country
Files series published by Franklin Watts. It is
produced for Franklin Watts by Bender
Richardson White, PO Box 266, Uxbridge, UK.
Editors: Lionel Bender, Angela Royston
Designer and Page Make-up: Ben White
Picture Researcher: Cathy Stastny
Cover Make-up: Mike Pilley, Radius
Production: Kim Richardson

Graphics and Maps: Stefan Chabluk
Educational Advisor: Prue Goodwin, Institute of
Education, The University of Reading
Consultant: Dr Terry Jennings, a former
geography teacher and university lecturer. He is
now a full-time writer of children's geography
and science books.

A CIP catalogue record for this book is available
from the British Library.

ISBN 0-7496-6033-3
Dewey Classification 917.29

Printed in China

Picture Credits

Pages 1: James Davis Travel Photography. 3: DAS
Photo/David Simson. 4: Hutchison Photo
Library/Philip Wolmuth. 6: DAS Photo/David Simson.
8: Hutchison Photo Library/Brian Moser. 10-11 bottom:
DAS Photo/David Simson. 11: DAS Photo/David
Simson. 12: DAS Photo/David Simson. 13: Hutchison
Photo Library/Errington. 14: DAS Photo/David Simson.
15: DAS Photo/David Simson. 16-17: Hutchison Photo
Library/Philip Wolmuth. 18: DAS Photo/David Simson.
19: Hutchison Photo Library/Jeremy Horner.
20: DAS Photo/David Simson. 21: DAS Photo/David
Simson. 22: James Davis Travel Photography.
22/23 bottom: Hutchison Photo Library/James
Henderson. 24: Corbis Images Inc/Philip Gould.
25: Corbis Images Inc/Jan Butchofsky. 27: DAS
Photo/David Simson. 29: Hutchison Photo
Library/James Henderson. 30: DAS Photo/David
Simson. 31: DAS Photo/David Simson.
Cover photo: Robert Harding Photo Library.

The Author

Ian Graham is a full-time
writer and editor of non-
fiction books. He has written
more than 100 books for
children.

Note to parents and teachers

Every effort has been made by the Publishers to ensure
that the websites in this book are suitable for children,
that they are of the highest educational value, and that
they contain no inappropriate or offensive material.
However, because of the nature of the Internet, it is
impossible to guarantee that the contents of these sites
will not be altered. We strongly advise that Internet
access is supervised by a responsible adult.

Contents

Welcome to the Caribbean

When people think of the Caribbean, they usually think of white beaches, palm trees and clear, blue water.

Chains of islands

The Caribbean includes all the islands in the Caribbean Sea. Most of the islands form three chains — the Greater Antilles, the Lesser Antilles and the Bahamas. The Caribbean also includes Guyana, which is part of South America, and the nearby islands of Trinidad and Tobago.

DATABASE

The Greater Antilles are four large islands – Cuba, Hispaniola (Haiti and Dominican Republic), Puerto Rico and Jamaica.

The Lesser Antilles are split into two groups – the Windward Islands and Leeward Islands.

The Caribbean is sometimes called the West Indies.

Below. **Soufrière is a fishing port on St Lucia. The island is one of the Windward Islands.**

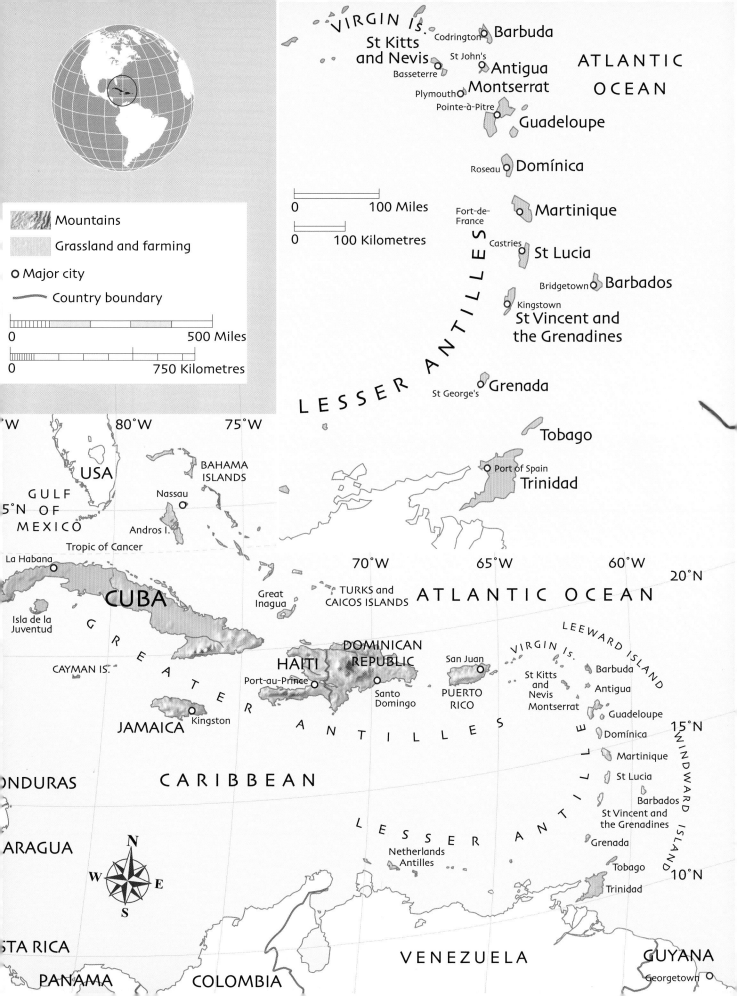

VIRGIN IS.
St Kitts
and Nevis
Codrington
Barbuda
St John's
Antigua
Basseterre
Montserrat
Plymouth
Pointe-à-Pitre
Guadeloupe

ATLANTIC
OCEAN

Roseau ○ Domínica

Fort-de-
France
Martinique

Castries
St Lucia

Bridgetown
Barbados

Kingstown
St Vincent and
the Grenadines

LESSER ANTILLES

St George's ○ Grenada

Tobago

○ Port of Spain
Trinidad

Legend

	Mountains
	Grassland and farming
○	Major city
	Country boundary

0 — 500 Miles
0 — 750 Kilometres

0 — 100 Miles
0 — 100 Kilometres

80°W   75°W

USA

BAHAMA
ISLANDS

Nassau

GULF OF MEXICO

25°N

Andros I.

Tropic of Cancer

La Habana

CUBA

Isla de la
Juventud

CAYMAN IS.

G R E A T E R

ATLANTIC OCEAN

20°N

70°W   65°W   60°W

TURKS and
CAICOS ISLANDS

Great
Inagua

DOMINICAN
REPUBLIC

HAITI

Port-au-Prince
Santo
Domingo

San Juan

PUERTO
RICO

VIRGIN IS.

LEEWARD ISLAND

St Kitts
and
Nevis
Montserrat

Barbuda

Antigua

Guadeloupe

Domínica

15°N

WINDWARD ISLAND

JAMAICA
Kingston

A N T I L L E S

Martinique

St Lucia

Barbados

St Vincent and
the Grenadines

ONDURAS

CARIBBEAN

L E S S E R   A N T I L L E S

Grenada

Tobago

Trinidad

10°N

ARAGUA

N
W   E
S

Netherlands
Antilles

STA RICA

VENEZUELA

GUYANA

PANAMA   COLOMBIA

Georgetown

The Land

The weather in the Caribbean is warm all year round. It is slightly cooler in the mountains and at night. It often rains very heavily.

Wet and stormy

The wettest weather is between June and November. During this time, some of the islands are very hot and damp. Hurricanes and storms can strike the islands at any time between July and October.

Volcanoes

Many of the Caribbean islands have volcanoes. Some of these are still active. Mount Soufrière on the island of St Vincent erupted in 1812, 1902, 1971 and 1979. The people had to leave the island until the danger was over. Other volcanoes have not erupted for a long time. The largest islands have the highest mountains.

Animal Life

All the Caribbean islands have lizards, snakes and colourful birds – especially parrots. Only Trinidad has monkeys and other mammals. The sea is filled with life, too. Coral reefs are home to more than 1,000 kinds of fish.

Below. **Coconut palms and many other plants grow on the island of St Vincent. The plants grow well because it rains a lot.**

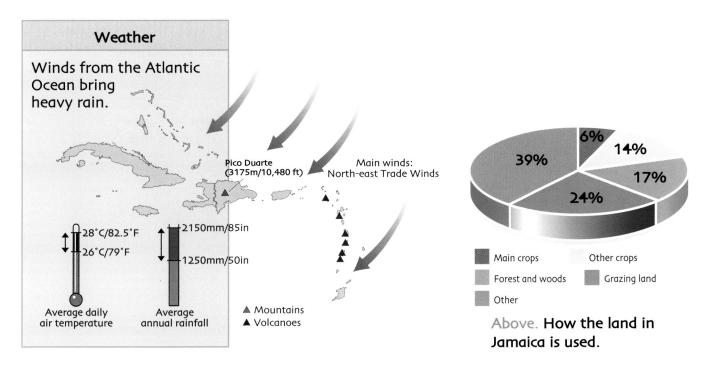

Weather

Winds from the Atlantic Ocean bring heavy rain.

Pico Duarte
(3175m/10,480 ft)

Main winds:
North-east Trade Winds

28°C/82.5°F
26°C/79°F

Average daily
air temperature

2150mm/85in
1250mm/50in

Average
annual rainfall

▲ Mountains
▲ Volcanoes

6%
14%
17%
24%
39%

Main crops
Other crops
Forest and woods
Grazing land
Other

Above. **How the land in Jamaica is used.**

Below. **Average rainfall each month in Kingston, Jamaica.**

Below. **Average temperatures in Kingston, Jamaica.**

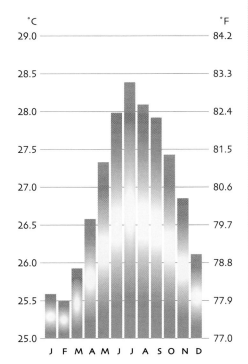

Web Search ▶▶

► www.barbados.org/
weather.htm
The weather and climate in Barbados.

► www.go-jamaica.com/
weather/ maps.php
The weather in Jamaica.

► www.caribwx.com/climate1.
html
The weather in British Virgin Islands.

► www.worldclimate.com
Facts and figures on world climate.

The People

The Caribbean is named after the Carib Indians. They were living in the Lesser Antilles when the first Spanish explorers invaded and took over the islands in the 15th century.

There are 36 million people living in the Caribbean today. Their ancestors came from all over the world.

Slave trading

Most Caribbeans have ancestors from West Africa. They were brought to the islands by European slave traders 300 to 400 years ago. The slaves worked on sugar plantations.

Below. **Caribbeans shop at a street market on Curaçao, an island in the Lesser Antilles.**

8

Asian ancestors

More people arrived in the Caribbean between 100 and 200 years ago. They came from India and China. Many of them still speak Hindi, Urdu and Chinese.

Main languages

Many Caribbeans speak Spanish, English, French or Dutch. These are the languages of the Europeans who colonized the islands. The slaves developed their own languages – pidgin and creole. Some Caribbean languages are made up of many languages.

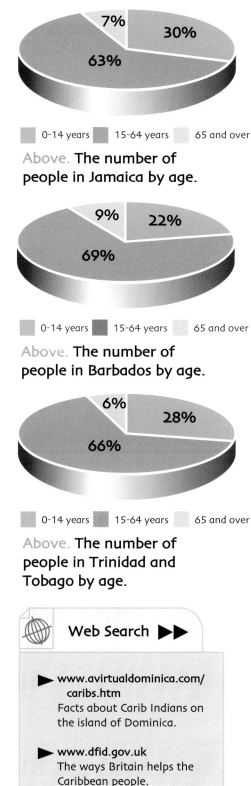

Above. **The number of people in Jamaica by age.**

Above. **The number of people in Barbados by age.**

Above. **The number of people in Trinidad and Tobago by age.**

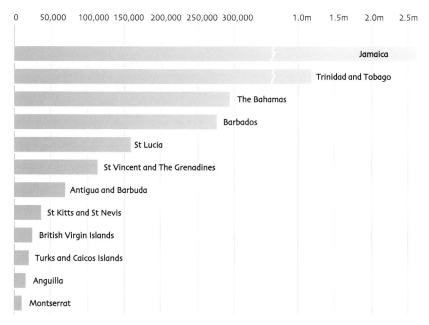

Above. **The number of people who live on some of the islands in the Caribbean.**

Web Search ▶▶

▶ www.avirtualdominica.com/caribs.htm
Facts about Carib Indians on the island of Dominica.

▶ www.dfid.gov.uk
The ways Britain helps the Caribbean people.

Town and Country Life

At one time, most people in the Caribbean worked on farms in the countryside. Now, more than half of its people live in towns and cities.

Living in the cities

During the last 100 years, many people left the countryside to find work in the towns and cities. Towns on the coast have become popular holiday places for tourists. Shanty towns have grown up around the cities. The people who live in shanty towns often have no electricity or clean water.

 **Kingston, Jamaica**

More than 500,000 people live in Kingston, the capital of Jamaica. Another 200,000 more people live in the suburbs around Kingston.

Jamaica became a British colony in 1655.

Kingston was founded in 1692. Its name means 'king's town' in honour of the British king at the time, William III.

Population of main cities

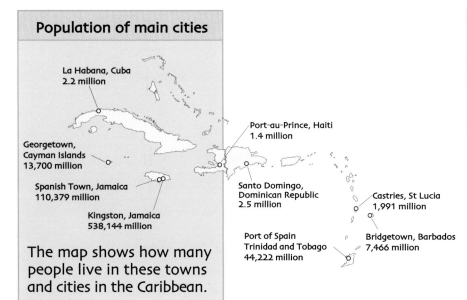

La Habana, Cuba
2.2 million

Georgetown,
Cayman Islands
13,700 million

Spanish Town, Jamaica
110,379 million

Kingston, Jamaica
538,144 million

Port-au-Prince, Haiti
1.4 million

Santo Domingo,
Dominican Republic
2.5 million

Castries, St Lucia
1,991 million

Port of Spain
Trinidad and Tobago
44,222 million

Bridgetown, Barbados
7,466 million

The map shows how many people live in these towns and cities in the Caribbean.

Left. This wooden shanty is in Sandy Bay, in Jamaica. More than a third of Jamaicans are poor.

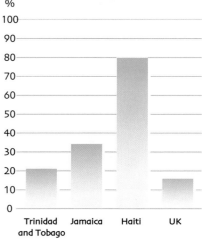

Above. Comparing the percentage of poor people in three Caribbean countries and in the United Kingdom.

Street Markets

People meet at the street markets. There people sell fruit and vegetables they have grown on their plots of land. This includes yams, plantains, bananas and squashes.

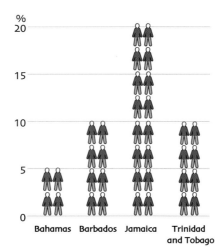

Above. The percentages of people who work in farming in four Caribbean countries.

Web Search ▶▶

▶ www.jis.gov.jm/water_ housing/index.asp
Information about housing in Jamaica.

▶ www.jis.gov.jm/land_environ ment/index.asp
The geography of Jamaica.

▶ www.unesco.org/focus/ indcarib.html
Caribbean population figures from the United Nations.

Left. Nassau, the capital of the Bahamas. Most towns and cities in the Caribbean grew larger and richer when they became tourist resorts.

Farming and Fishing

The Caribbean's warm, wet weather is very good for growing crops. But its storms can destroy the crops in minutes.

Main crops

Sugar-cane, bananas, coffee beans, tobacco and cocoa are the main crops grown in the Caribbean. They are grown on plantations, and are sold all over the world. People who live in the countryside also grow other plants and keep animals on their plots of land.

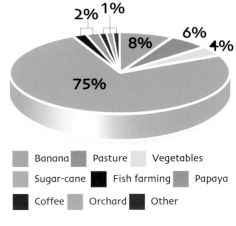

2% 1% 6% 4% 8% 75%

Banana	Pasture	Vegetables
Sugar-cane	Fish farming	Papaya
Coffee	Orchard	Other

Above. **Areas of land and lakes used for different kinds of farming.**

Fishing

The Caribbean Sea is full of fish, but most of them are small and swim around coral reefs. Fishermen catch large amounts of fish in only a few places.

Making pure sugar

1. Crush stalks of sugar-cane to make sap.
2. Leave sap in tanks to clear.
3. Boil sap to make a thick syrup.
4. Dry syrup to make brown sugar.
5. Refine brown sugar to get white sugar.

Left. **This plantation on St Lucia grows thousands of tonnes of bananas each year.**

Above. A fisherman near the coast of Grenada holds up a puffer fish that was trapped in his net. This fish will be returned to the sea.

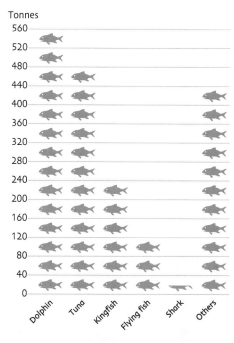

Above. Weights of different kinds of fish caught by boats from St Lucia.

Farming and Fishing

Large amounts of fish are mostly caught around the Bahamas.

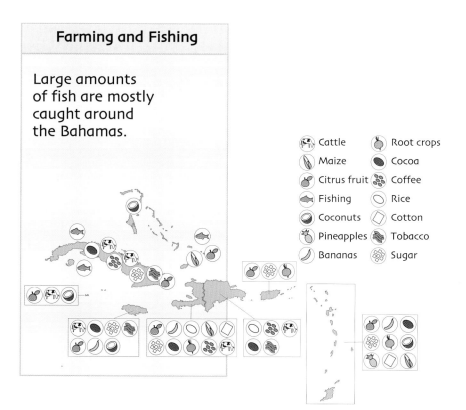

Cattle
Maize
Citrus fruit
Fishing
Coconuts
Pineapples
Bananas
Root crops
Cocoa
Coffee
Rice
Cotton
Tobacco
Sugar

Web Search ▶▶

▶ www.cbea.org
The Caribbean Banana Exporters Association.

▶ www.jamaicancoffee.gov.jm
Information about Jamaica's coffee industry.

▶ www.caricom–fisheries.com/
Fishing industry of many Caribbean countries.

Resources and Industry

The Caribbean makes most of its money from tourism and selling its crops, oil and metals to other countries.

Tourism

For some islands, tourism is the main industry. Tourists enjoy the beaches, the scenery and the hot, sunny weather.

Generating Electricity

Most electricity in the Caribbean is produced by burning coal, oil and gas. Hydroelectricity is also important. It uses the energy of flowing water to make electricity.

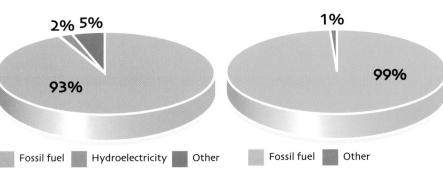

2% 5%

93%

■ Fossil fuel ■ Hydroelectricity ■ Other

Above. **How electricity is produced in Jamaica.**

1%

99%

■ Fossil fuel ■ Other

Above. **How electricity is produced in Trinidad and Tobago.**

Above. **Bauxite is rich in aluminium. Jamaica mines and produces over 11,000 tonnes of bauxite a year.**

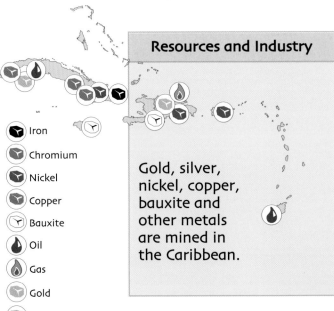

Resources and Industry

Gold, silver, nickel, copper, bauxite and other metals are mined in the Caribbean.

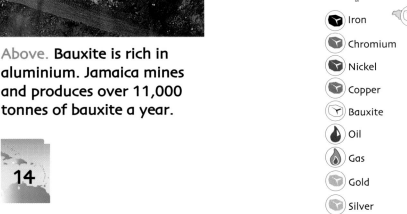

Iron
Chromium
Nickel
Copper
Bauxite
Oil
Gas
Gold
Silver

Sugar trade

Europeans set up large plantations to grow sugar-cane on many of the islands in the Caribbean. Some sugar is made into rum, an alcoholic drink. Most of the sugar and rum are sold to European countries.

Other industries

Caribbean countries also make clothes and furniture, and mine metals. The Bahamas and Trinidad and Tobago have oil wells. Some of the oil is made into different kinds of plastic.

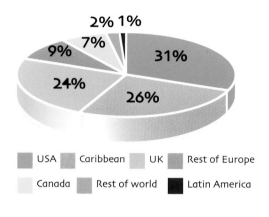

| USA | Caribbean | UK | Rest of Europe |
| Canada | Rest of world | Latin America |

Above. **Where tourists visiting St Lucia come from.**

Below. **The Caribbean's tropical climate makes it popular with tourists. Many sail from island to island on huge, expensive cruise ships.**

Web Search ▶▶

▶ **www.gov.tt**
Trinidad and Tobago government information.

▶ **www.stats.gov.lc**
St Lucia government facts and figures.

▶ **www.caribtourism.com**
Tourism in the Caribbean.

Transport

It is easy to travel to and around the Caribbean. Most islands have an airport and good harbours for yachts and ferries. There are also docks for international cargo ships.

Planes

Most islands have international airports with flights to Europe and the United States. Island-hoppers are small planes that fly between the islands from small airports.

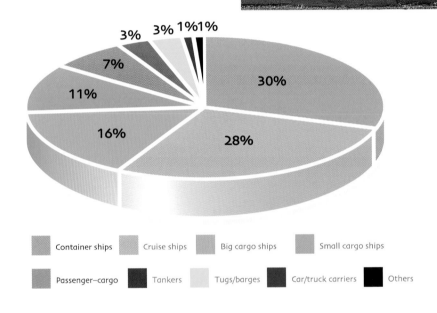

Container ships   Cruise ships   Big cargo ships   Small cargo ships

Passenger–cargo   Tankers   Tugs/barges   Car/truck carriers   Others

Above. The kinds of ships that sail to St Lucia each year.

'000   0   1   2   3   4   5   6   7   8   9   10   11   12   13   14

Private vehicles

Goods vehicles

Passenger buses & vans

Taxis/hired vehicles

Motorcycles

Other

Left. The kinds and numbers of road vehicles used on St Lucia. One symbol represents 1,000 vehicles.

Road Traffic

On islands that were colonized by Britain, vehicles drive on the left side of the road, as they do in Britain. These islands include Jamaica, Barbados, Trinidad and Tobago and the British Virgin Islands. On the islands colonized by other European countries, vehicles drive on the right side of the road.

Road and rail

Towns and cities have modern, tarmacked roads. In the countryside, many roads are dirt tracks. Most islands have buses and taxis. A few islands have railways, too. They are used mainly by the sugar plantations and mines.

Web Search ▶▶

www.mtw.gov.jm
The Jamaican Ministry of Transport and Works.

www.stats.gov.lc/index7.htm
Facts and figures for vehicles on St Lucia.

www.trinbagoinfo.com/trinbagoinfo/TrinidadandTobagoTransportation.htm
Information about airports and flights for Trinidad and Tobago.

www.airjamaica.com
The website of Air Jamaica.

Transport

The main airports and sea routes in the Caribbean.

 International airports
Shipping lanes

Education

Most schools in the Caribbean are free and are run by the government. The larger islands have a few private schools, which charge fees to parents.

Primary school

Children start school when they are four or five years old. On some Caribbean islands, school starts at 7.30 a.m. and finishes at 2.00 p.m.

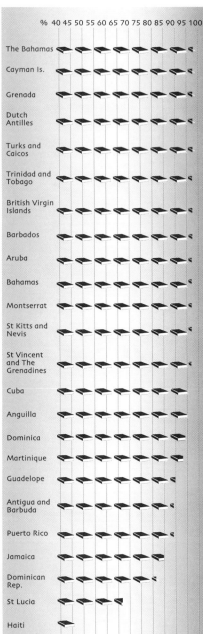

%	40 45 50 55 60 65 70 75 80 85 90 95 100
The Bahamas	
Cayman Is.	
Grenada	
Dutch Antilles	
Turks and Caicos	
Trinidad and Tobago	
British Virgin Islands	
Barbados	
Aruba	
Bahamas	
Montserrat	
St Kitts and Nevis	
St Vincent and The Grenadines	
Cuba	
Anguilla	
Dominica	
Martinique	
Guadelope	
Antigua and Barbuda	
Puerto Rico	
Jamaica	
Dominican Rep.	
St Lucia	
Haiti	

Above. The percentages of people on some of the islands who can read.

Left. A secondary-school student in Barbados looks through a microscope during a science lesson.

Secondary school

Children go to secondary school when they are 11 years old. There they study languages, maths, science, art and other subjects. When children are 16, they sit the Caribbean Examination Council (CXC) exams. At age 18 they may sit the Advanced Level exams.

University

The main university is the University of the West Indies. It is based mainly in Jamaica, Barbados and Trinidad, but there are smaller branches on other islands, too.

Above. **Pupils at a primary school in St Lucia. Most school children in the Caribbean wear a uniform.**

Web Search ▶▶

www.cabinet.gov.jm/docs/MinEdCulture.htm
The Jamaican Ministry of Education and Culture.

www.uwimona.edu.jm
The University of West Indies Mona campus.

www.ncu.edu.jm
Northern Caribbean University.

Sport and Leisure

Caribbean sportsmen and sportswomen are among the best in the world. The Jamaican netball team is becoming as famous as the West Indies' cricket team. Football is popular, too.

Olympic Games

Caribbean athletes take part in many events. In spite of the Caribbean's warm climate, the Jamaican bobsleigh team competed in three Winter Olympic Games.

Test Cricket

International cricket matches are known as test matches. Between 1970 and 1980, the West Indies cricket team was the best in the world. It lost only two of the test matches that it played.

Below. **Horse-racing at Bridgetown in Barbados.**

DATABASE

Famous West Indian cricketers include:
• Curtly Ambrose (Antigua)
• Brian Lara (Trinidad)
• Clive Lloyd (Guyana)
• Sir Vivian Richards (Antigua)
• Sir Garfield 'Gary' Sobers (Barbados)

Athletes include:
• Donovan Bailey (Jamaica)
• Merlene Ottey (Jamaica)

Left. Many children like to play cricket. Here, one boy gets ready to bat. The other boy is the wicket-keeper.

 Web Search ▶▶

www.top5jamaica.com/sports.html
All about Jamaican sports.

www.westindies.cricinfo.com
Cricket in the West Indies.

www.jamaicans.com/bobsled/
The Jamaican bobsleigh team.

Leisure

Tourists and local people enjoy many sports and activities. Water sports include diving, snorkelling, windsurfing, parasailing and swimming. People also hike, rock climb and go horse riding.

Daily Life and Religion

Everyday life in the Caribbean is busy and noisy, especially in the towns and cities. Religion is important to many Caribbean people.

Daily life

Life varies from island to island and between the city and the countryside. Each day, people shop for food, usually in markets.

Left. **This fruit market is in St George's, the capital of Grenada.**

22

European religions

Most Caribbean people are Christian. On islands colonized by Spain and France, many people are Catholic. On islands colonized by Britain, most people are Protestant.

Other religions

Many people, especially in Trinidad, are Hindu or Muslim. Rastafarianism is a religion popular in Jamaica. It praises the Ethiopian emperor, Haile Selassie. Voodoo mixes Roman Catholic and African beliefs.

Below. **Protestants hold services every Sunday in this parish church in Mandeville, in Jamaica.**

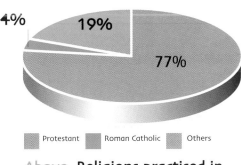

4% 19% 77%

Protestant   Roman Catholic   Others

Above. **Religions practised in Barbados.**

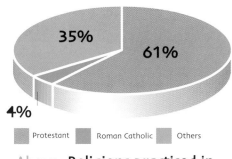

35% 61% 4%

Protestant   Roman Catholic   Others

Above. **Religions practised in Jamaica.**

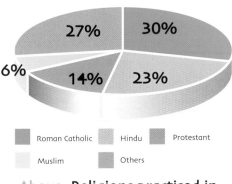

27% 30% 6% 14% 23%

Roman Catholic   Hindu   Protestant
Muslim   Others

Above. **Religions practised in Trinidad and Tobago.**

Web Search ▶▶

www.barbados.org/churches.htm
Information on the different churches in Barbados.

www.moh.gov.jm/
The Jamaican Ministry of Health.

Arts and Media

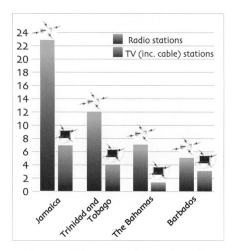

Above. **The number of radio and television stations on four Caribbean islands or island groups.**

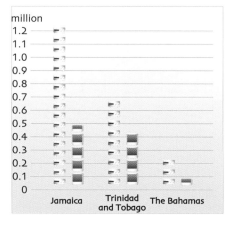

Above. **The number of people on these Caribbean islands who own televisions and radios.**

Right. **Carnival time in Martinique. People dress up and dance in the streets.**

Music and dance are a big part of Caribbean culture. Many Caribbean writers are well-known and respected all over the world.

Music

Reggae, calypso and steel band music all began in the Caribbean. The music is based on rhythms, melodies and stories that the slaves brought with them from Africa. Steel bands began in Trinidad in the 1930s. The top of a drum is hammered into shapes that each make a different sound when they are hit with a drumstick.

Above. **Steel bands are popular all year round on many islands in the Caribbean.**

Newspapers

Most islands have their own newspapers. Newspapers in most Caribbean countries are free to criticize the government.

Radio and television

Some television and radio stations are owned by the government. Others are privately owned. People can watch satellite and cable television from the United States.

Famous Caribbean Writers

V S Naipaul (born in Trinidad in 1932) has written several novels set in the Caribbean.

Derek Walcott (born in St. Lucia in 1930) won the Nobel Prize for Literature in 1992. He writes poetry and plays.

Samuel Selvon (1923-94) wrote about the lives and experiences of Indian immigrants to the Caribbean.

Andrew Salkey (1928-95) wrote plays, novels and poems about Jamaica.

 **Web Search ▶▶**

▶ www.sbgmusic.com/html/ teacher/reference/cultures/ jamaica.html
The development of Jamaican song and dance.

▶ www.jamaicaobserver.com
Website of the *Jamaica Observer* newspaper.

▶ www.guardian.co.tt
Trinidad Guardian newspaper.

www.thenassauguardian.com
▶ *Nassau Guardian* newspaper, Bahamas.

Government

Most countries in the Caribbean are ruled by governments that the people vote for every few years.

Independence

During the 1960s and 1970s, most Caribbean countries became independent. This means that they were no longer ruled by the European countries that had colonized them. However, many countries still keep close links with their former rulers.

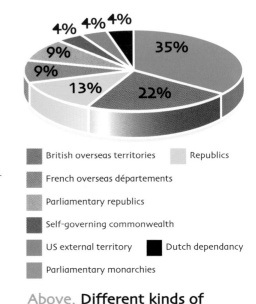

- British overseas territories
- French overseas départements
- Parliamentary republics
- Self-governing commonwealth
- US external territory
- Parliamentary monarchies
- Republics
- Dutch dependancy

Above. **Different kinds of government in the Caribbean.**

Invasion

In Grenada in 1979, the army overthrew the country's government. In 1983, a military force led by the United States invaded the island. The people of Grenada then elected a new government.

Right. **The type of government in different countries in the Caribbean.**

Government status of some Caribbean countries

Country	Status	Since
Antigua and Barbuda	Parliamentary monarchy	1981
Bahamas	Parliamentary monarchy	1973
Barbados	Parliamentary monarchy	1966
British Virgin Islands	British overseas territory	1960
Cuba	Republic	1898
Dominican Republic	Republic	1865
Grenada	Parliamentary monarchy	1974
Guadeloupe	French overseas département	1946
Guyana	Parliamentary republic	1966
Haiti	Republic	1804
Jamaica	Parliamentary monarchy	1962
Montserrat	British overseas territory	1960
Puerto Rico	Self-governing commonwealth	1952
St. Kitts and Nevis	Parliamentary monarchy	1983
St. Lucia	Parliamentary monarchy	1979
Trinidad and Tobago	Parliamentary republic	1962
Turks and Caicos Islands	British overseas territory	1972
US Virgin Islands	US external territory	1917

A monarchy has a king or queen as head of state.
A republic is led by a president – if there is a royal family, it has no power.
A département or an external or overseas territory is still partly governed by the original ruling country.

Kinds of government

Many countries that were once British colonies became parliamentary monarchies. This means they elect their own parliament but have the British monarch as their head of state. Parliamentary republics elect their own parliament, too, but elect a president as head of state. Some countries are British Overseas Territories. They elect their own government, but they have a governor who is appointed by Britain.

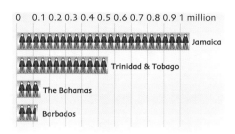

0 0.1 0.2 0.3 0.4 0.5 0.6 0.7 0.8 0.9 1 million

Jamaica

Trinidad & Tobago

The Bahamas

Barbados

Above. **The number of workers in some of the main Caribbean countries.**

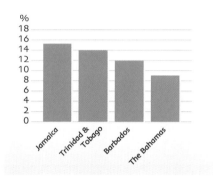

Above. **Workers in these islands who do not have work.**

Below. **A soldier stands on guard outside the government offices in Nassau in the Bahamas.**

Web Search ▶▶

▶ www.gov.tt
The government of Trinidad and Tobago.

▶ www.stlucia.gov.lc
The government of St Lucia.

▶ www.caribinfo.com/govern ment.html
Information about all the Caribbean governments.

Place in the World

Historical Events until the 1970s

1000
Carib Indians settle in the Windward Islands

1498
Christopher Columbus reaches Trinidad

1510
Spain occupies Jamaica

1620s
St Kitts becomes Britain's first Caribbean colony

1627
British colonists arrive on Barbados

1637
Sugar-cane first grown in Barbados

1655
Britain takes Jamaica from Spain

1834
Slavery abolished in British Caribbean

1960s
Many islands gain independence

1968
Caribbean Free Trade Association (CARIFTA) is formed

Caribbean countries are members of many international organizations. They also trade with each other and with the rest of the world.

International organizations

Countries in the Caribbean belong to many organizations, including the United Nations (UN) and the International Olympic Committee. Many Caribbean countries joined an organization for former British colonies called the Commonwealth.

Below. **The flags of some of the main Caribbean countries.**

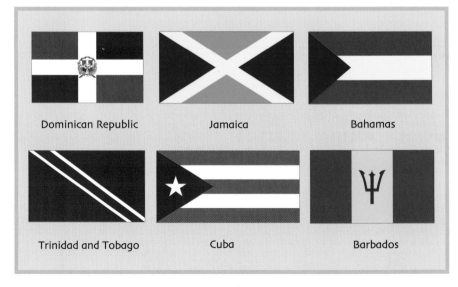

Dominican Republic   Jamaica   Bahamas

Trinidad and Tobago   Cuba   Barbados

Above. **The Palais de Justice (Law Courts) at Port de France on Martinique. People in Martinique and Guadeloupe have to obey French laws and elect representatives to the French parliament in Paris.**

Trade

The Caribbean Community and Common Market (CARICOM) is an organization that helps Caribbean countries trade with each other. Most international trade used to be with the European countries that colonized the Caribbean. Now, most international trade is with the United States.

Below. **Total money earned on some Caribbean islands.**

Below. **Money earned from exports from some Caribbean islands.**

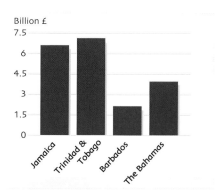

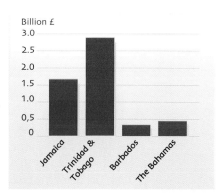

DATABASE

Historical Events since the 1970s

1970s
Many other islands gain independence

1981
The Organization of Eastern Caribbean States formed

1982
Anguilla becomes a British Dependent Territory

1983
St Kitts and Nevis gains independence

1997
Volcanic eruptions on Montserrat destroy town of Plymouth

2000
More volcanic eruptions on Montserrat

Web Search ▶▶

▶ www.oecs.org
The Organization of Eastern Caribbean States.

▶ www.jftc.com
Jamaica Fair Trading Commission.

▶ www.caricom.org
Caribbean Community and Common Market.

These figures are for Jamaica, the Bahamas, Barbados and Trinidad and Tobago.

Total area: 30,488 sq km

Total population: 4,397,734

Capital cities:
Kingston, Jamaica (population 538,144)
Nassau, Bahamas (172,196)
Bridgetown, Barbados (7,466)
Port-of-Spain, Trinidad and Tobago (44,222)

Longest river:
Black River, Jamaica (71 km)

Highest mountain:
Blue Mountain Peak, Jamaica (2,256 m)

Jamaica's flag:
A gold diagonal cross with two black and two green triangles. Gold is for the island's natural wealth and sunlight; green, hope and farming resources; the black, hardships overcome

Official language:
English

Currencies:
Jamaican dollar (J$), Bahamian dollar (B$), Barbadian dollar (Bds$), Trinidad and Tobago dollar (TT$)

Major resources:
Bauxite, gypsum, limestone, natural gas, petroleum, asphalt, salt, timber

Major exports:
Bauxite, sugar, rum, alumina, bananas, coffee, cocoa, cement

Some public holidays:
1 January: New Year's Day
Mid-February to early March: Carnival, Trinidad and Tobago
Late March to late April: Good Friday, Easter Monday
1 May: Labour Day, Barbados
23 May: Labour Day, Jamaica
1st Friday in June: Labour Day, Bahamas
19 June: Labour Day, Trinidad and Tobago
10 July: Independence Day, Bahamas
1st Monday in August: Independence Day, Jamaica
31 August: Independence Day, Trinidad and Tobago
16 October: National Heroes' Day, Jamaica
30 November: Independence Day, Barbados
25 December: Christmas Day

Main religions:
Protestantism, Roman Catholicism, Hinduism, Islam, Rastafarianism, Voodoo

Key Words

ANCESTOR
A grandparent or other relative from whom you are descended.

CARGO
Goods or products carried in a ship, airplane or lorry.

CLIMATE
The kind of weather a place usually has at different times of the year.

COLONY
A country ruled by another country.

EXPORTS
Goods sold to a foreign country.

FOSSIL FUEL
A fuel such as coal, oil or natural gas that has formed from the bodies of plants and animals that died millions of years ago.

GOVERNMENT
The organization that runs a country.

HURRICANE
A powerful, destructive storm; hurricane-force winds blow at more than 160 kph.

IMMIGRANTS
People coming to live and work in a country from other countries.

INDEPENDENT
Ruled by people living in the country and not by another country.

MEDICAL SERVICES
Hospitals, doctors and organizations that keep people healthy and look after sick people.

PARLIAMENT
A group of people elected to represent the people and make new laws in a country.

PLANTATION
An area of farmland on which trees or shrubs are grown for their fruit or leaves.

REPUBLIC
A form of government, usually led by a president, in which people are elected.

RESOURCES
The raw materials, land and people's skills that a country uses to make money.

SHANTY
A house of poor people made out of waste material.

TOURISM
The industry involving tourists, hotels, beach resorts.

TRADE
Buying and selling goods.

TROPICAL
The part of the Earth that lies each side of the Equator; tropical can also mean very warm or hot and damp, like the climate in the tropics.

Index